NINJA FOODI OR
DUAL ZONE *Air Fryer*
with Colors

COOKBOOK

BY: ALEXANDRA BALFE

Table of Contents

BREAKFAST

01 Aubergine Sandwich, Italian Style

02 Frittata with Roasted Peppers

03 Crispy Fried Mushrooms

04 Bowls of Tofu and Quinoa

05 Fluffy Pancakes

06 Toast with Pesto Spread

LUNCH

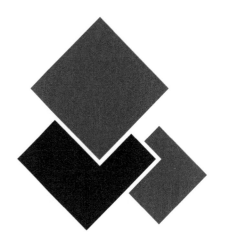

07 Amazing Pizza Morsels

08 Air-Fried 'Hard-Cooked' Eggs

09 Crispy Chicken Drumettes

10 Flavorful Cod in Curry Sauce

11 Traditional Turkish Meatballs

12 Savoury Herb Chicken

POULTRY

13 Spiced Cinnamon-Infused Chicken

14 Savory Chicken Thighs with Aromatic Rice

15 Citrus-Infused Garlic Chicken

16 Fig-Sauced Turkey Delight

17 Herbed Tarragon Chicken Breast

18 Duck Breast in Rich Tomato Glaze

MEAT

19 BBQ Chicken Cooked in Air Fryer

20 Beef Prepared in Chinese Fashion

21 Meatballs Made from Lamb

22 Beef Kabobs Cooked in an Air Fryer

23 Beef with Arugula and Leeks

24 Lamb Patties Made in an Air Fryer

SEAFOOD

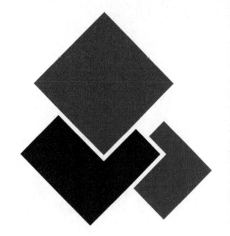

25 Air Fryer Fish & Chips

26 Rosemary Shrimp Kabobs

27 Air Fryer Tilapia

28 Roasted Cod and Parsley

29 Black Cod with Grapes, Fennel, Pecans and Kale

30 Coconut Shrimp

SIDE DISH

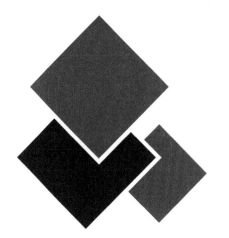

31   Air-Fryer Carrots

32   Yellow Squash and courgette

33   Air-Fryer Potato Wedges

34   Air-Fryer Hash Browns

35   Moroccan Aubergine Dish

36   Garlic Potatoes

STARTERS

37 Fantastic Potato Chips

38 Maple Parsnips

39 runner beans Roasted

40 Mayo Brussels Sprouts

41 Air-Fryer Plantains

42 Endives and Rice

VEGETABLE

43 Air-Fryer Baked Potato

44 Simple Aubergine

45 courgette Fries

46 Dill Corn

47 Stuffed Sweet Potatoes

48 Air-Fryer Red Potatoes

DESSERTS

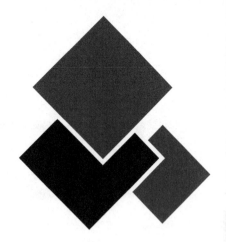

49 Strawberry Jam

50 Pumpkin Cookies

51 Healthy Banana Bread

52 Creamy White Chocolate Cheesecake

53 Creamy White Chocolate Cheesecake

54 Plum Bars Recipe

Recipes

BREAKFAST

Aubergine Sandwich, Italian Style

Cook time
55 Minutes

Servings: 4

Ingredients

- A sliced Aubergine
- 60g panko breadcrumbs
- Four bread slices
- 120g mayonnaise
- 180g tomato paste
- 2g garlic powder
- 2g parsley; chopped

- 2g Italian seasoning
- 15ml avocado oil + a drizzle
- 30ml coconut milk
- 8g fresh basil; chopped
- 15g cheddar cheese; grated
- 240g mozzarella cheese; grated
- Salt and black pepper

Directions

1. After adding salt and pepper to the Aubergine slices, let them sit for around thirty minutes.

2. After that, wipe them dry and give them a milk and mayo brush. Stir together the salt, breadcrumbs, black pepper, Italian seasoning, garlic powder, and parsley in a bowl.

3. Then, coat the Aubergine slices with this mixture and arrange them on a baking sheet that has been prepared. Drizzle with oil. After inserting the baking sheet into the air fryer's basket, cook the Aubergine slices for a quarter-hour at 205°C, turning them halfway through. Apply the last tablespoon of oil to the bread slices. Next, place two of them on a work surface, cover with tomato paste, cooked Aubergine pieces, mozzarella, cheddar, and basil, and then place the other two bread slices on top.

4. After ten minutes of grilling sandwiches, serve.

Frittata with Roasted Peppers

Cook time
"à Minutes

Servings: 4

Ingredients

- 170g jarred roasted red peppers; chopped.
- 50g parmesan cheese; grated
- Twelve whisked eggs
- Three minced garlic cloves
- 6g parsley; chopped.

- 6g chives; chopped.
- 90g ricotta cheese
- A drizzle of olive oil
- Salt and black pepper

Directions

2

1. Whisk together the peppers, salt, garlic, parsley, chives, pepper, ricotta, and eggs in a mixing bowl.

2. Preheat your air fryer device to 150°C; after that, add the oil and spread it.

3. Cook for around twenty minutes after adding the egg mixture, spreading it evenly, and don't forget to top it with parmesan.

4. Serve on individual plates.

Crispy Fried Mushrooms

Cook time
25 Minutes

Servings: 3

Ingredients

- 230g spinach; torn
- Four-halved cherry tomatoes
- Four chopped slices of beef bacon
- Four eggs

- Eight sliced white mushrooms
- A minced garlic clove
- A drizzle of olive oil
- Salt and black pepper

Directions

3

1. In an oiled pan that suits your air fryer device, mix all of the items except for the spinach and stir well.
2. Insert the pan into your air fryer and cook for a quarter-hour at 205°C.
3. Give it an additional five minutes of cooking after adding the spinach. Divide among platters and serve.

Bowls of Tofu and Quinoa

Cook time
24 Minutes

Servings: 4

Ingredients

- 455g fresh romanesco; torn
- 340g firm tofu; cubed
- 225g baby spinach; torn
- Three chopped carrots

- A chopped red pepper; chopped.
- 60g soy sauce
- 360g red quinoa; cooked
- 60ml maple syrup
- 30ml olive oil
- 30ml lime juice

Directions

1. Combine the tofu, oil, soy sauce, lime juice, and maple syrup in your air fryer machine.
2. Simmer at 175°C for fifteen minutes, stirring midway, then pour into a bowl.
3. Toss in spinach, peppers, quinoa, carrots, and romanesco.
4. Divide into bowls. Present and savour.

Fluffy Pancakes

Cook time
30 Minutes

Servings: 4

Ingredients

- 218g white flour
- 125g apple; peeled, cored and chopped.
- 1¼ cups milk
- A whisked egg

- 30g sugar
- 10g baking powder
- 1.25g vanilla extract
- 5g cinnamon powder
- Cooking spray

Directions

5

1. Integrate all of the elements (except cooking spray) in a bowl and combine until a smooth batter is performed.
2. Use the cooking spray to grease your air fryer's pan, and after that, spread 1/4 of the batter into the pan.
3. Begin the cooking process for five minutes at 180°C, turning halfway through.
4. Duplicate steps 2 and 3 with 1/4 of the batter three more times, and then serve the pancakes directly.

Toast with Pesto Spread

Cook time
13 Minutes

Servings: 3

Ingredients

- Six bread slices
- Three garlic cloves; minced
- 240g mozzarella cheese; grated

- 30g basil and tomato pesto
- 70g butter; melted

Directions

6

1. On your working surface, place slices of bread.

2. Combine the garlic, butter, and pesto in a bowl, then spread it over each slice of bread.

3. Set them in the air fryer's basket, top with cheese, and cook for approximately 8 mins at 175°C. Serve immediately.

Recipes

LUNCH

Amazing Pizza Morsels

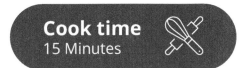

Cook time
15 Minutes

Servings: 4

Ingredients

- Two sheets of frozen puff pastry
- 70g pizza sauce
- 80g shredded salmon

- 227g can pineapple chunks in juice, drained
- 70g shredded pizza cheese

Directions

7

1. Start by preheating the air fryer to 200°C. Grease a baking tray that fits your device.
2. From each pastry sheet, cut 9 discs utilising a 7cm circular cutter.
3. Transfer to the ready tray. Evenly spread the pizza sauce
4. . Add cheese, chicken and pineapple on top. Bake until cheese is melted and the base is crunchy, about 15 minutes.

Air-Fried 'Hard-Cooked' Eggs

Cook time
02 Minutes

Servings: 3

Ingredients

- Four eggs

Directions

8

1. Gently put the eggs inside your air fryer basket. Preheat to 120°C. After removing the eggs from the basket using a big spoon, put them in a dish of cold water and let them sit for about two minutes.

2. Set the eggs in egg cups, cut off the tops, and serve for soft, medium-cooked eggs.

3. Gently tap the wide end of the egg on the bench to crack the shell, then peel it off in small pieces for medium- and hard-boiled eggs.

Crispy Chicken Drumettes

Cook time
50 Minutes

Servings: 3

Ingredients

- 1361g chicken wings
- 110g potato starch
- 115g butter; melted

- 15g Old Bay seasoning
- 5ml lemon juice

Directions

9

1. Arrange the chicken wings in the basket of your air fryer device after tossing them with the starch and Old Bay seasoning in a bowl. Cook for thirty-five minutes while occasionally shaking the fryer at 180 degrees Celsius.

2. Raise the heat to 205°C and continue cooking the chicken wings for a further 10 minutes.

3. After dividing the wings among plates, sprinkle each one with a mixture of melted butter and lemon juice.

Flavorful Cod in Curry Sauce

Cook time
24 Minutes

Servings: 3

Ingredients

- Four cod fillets; skinless, boneless and cubed
- 355ml milk; heated up
- 6g coriander; chopped.
- 5g ginger; grated
- 10g curry paste
- Salt and black pepper

Directions

1. Whisk together the salt, ginger, curry paste, ginger, and pepper in a bowl.
2. Place the fish in the pan that is compatible with your air fryer, then add the curry mix and milk and stir gently. Cook the pan in the fryer for 15 minutes at 205°C, shaking it halfway through.
3. Spoon the curry into individual bowls, garnish with coriander, and serve.

Traditional Turkish Meatballs

Cook time
25 MINS

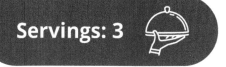
Servings: 3

Ingredients

- 30g feta cheese; crumbled
- 227g lean beef; minced
- 8g cumin; ground
- 1g mint; chopped

- A chopped leek
- 2g chopped parsley
- 1g minced garlic
- Salt and black pepper

Directions

II

1. Combine the beef, garlic, cheese, parsley, mint, leek, cumin, salt, and pepper in a bowl.
2. Stir thoroughly, followed by shaping the kofta mixture on sticks. Koftas should be cooked for about fifteen minutes in an air fryer that has been preheated to 180°C.
3. Serve and enjoy!!

Savoury Herb Chicken

Cook time
30 MINS

Servings: 3

Ingredients

- Two chicken breasts; skinless, boneless and cubed
- Eight sliced button mushrooms
- A chopped red pepper
- 15ml olive oil

- Six bread slices
- 1g thyme; dried
- 283g alfredo sauce
- 30g soft butter

Directions

12

1. Mix chicken, pepper, mushrooms, and oil in your air fryer device; toss to combine thoroughly. Cook for around 15 minutes at 160 °C.

2. Move the chicken mixture into a bowl and stir in the thyme and Alfredo sauce, then put it back in the air fryer to cook for an additional 4 minutes at 160°C.

3. Butter the bread slices, place them in the fryer, butter side up, and cook for an additional four minutes. Set slices of toast bread on a tray, cover with the chicken mixture, and serve for lunch.

Recipes

POULTRY

Spiced Cinnamon-Infused Chicken

Cook time
45 Minutes

Servings: 3

Ingredients

- 240ml chicken stock
- A whole chicken; cut into pieces
- 3g cinnamon powder
- 12g. garlic powder

- 15g olive oil
- 10g lemon zest
- 10g coriander powder
- Salt and black pepper to taste

Directions

1. In a bowl, merge all of the elements and stir well.
2. Set the chicken in the basket of your air fryer device, and cook it for 35 minutes at 175°C while occasionally shaking the fryer.
3. Serve the chicken with a side salad after dividing it among the plates.

Savory Chicken Thighs with Aromatic Rice

Cook time
30 Minutes

Servings: 3

Ingredients

- Three chopped carrots
- Four minced garlic cloves
- 2 lbs. chicken thighs; boneless and skinless
- 907g white rice
- 190ml red wine vinegar

- 60ml chicken stock
- 60ml olive oil
- 8g garlic powder
- 8g Italian seasoning
- 3g turmeric powder
- Salt and black pepper

Directions

14

1. Add all the ingredients to a pan that is compatible with your air fryer device and toss.

2. Insert the pan into the fryer and cook for half an hour at 175 degrees.

3. After dividing among plates, serve.

Citrus-Infused Garlic Chicken

Cook time
25 Minutes

Servings: 3

Ingredients

- Four chicken breasts; skinless and boneless
- Four garlic heads; peeled, cloves separated and cut into quarters
- 30ml lemon juice
- 2g lemon pepper
- 22ml avocado oil
- Salt and black pepper

Directions

1. Combine all of the elements in a bowl and well toss.
2. After moving the chicken mixture to your air fryer device, cook it for approximately 15 minutes at 180°C.
3. Divide among plates and come with a side salad.

15

Fig-Sauced Turkey Delight

Cook time
40 Minutes

Servings: 5

Ingredients

- Two halved turkey breasts
- A chopped shallot
- 240 mL chicken stock
- 120ml cranberry juice
- 15ml olive oil

- 2g garlic powder
- 1g sweet paprika
- 45g butter; melted
- 15g white flour
- 60g figs; chopped.
- Salt and black pepper

Directions

16

1. Over medium-high heat, put a pan with 1½ tablespoons of butter and olive oil.

2. Stir in the shallots and simmer for a couple of minutes. Stir in the figs, stock, cranberry juice, garlic powder, and paprika. Cook for seven to eight minutes.

3. After that, add the flour and cook for a further one to two minutes before turning off the heat. After adding salt and pepper to the turkey, cover it with the remaining 1½ tablespoons of butter.

4. Next, transfer the turkey to the basket of your air fryer device, then cook it for 15 minutes at 195°C, turning it halfway through.

5. Divide among dishes, cover with sauce, and proceed to serve.

Herbed Tarragon Chicken Breast

Cook time
25 Minutes

Servings: 3

Ingredients

- Two chicken breasts; skinless and boneless
- Two minced garlic cloves
- Eight chopped tarragon sprigs
- 240ml lemon juice
- 60ml soy sauce
- 15g. butter; melted
- Salt and black pepper

Directions

17

1. Combine the chicken with the salt, soy sauce, garlic, tarragon, pepper, butter, and lemon juice in a bowl; toss thoroughly and leave aside for ten minutes.
2. Move the marinated chicken to a baking dish that matches inside your air fryer machine, and cook it for 15 minutes at 175°C, shaking the fryer halfway through.
3. After dividing everything among the plates, serve.

Duck Breast in Rich Tomato Glaze

Cook time
25 Minutes
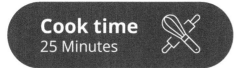

Servings: 3

Ingredients

- Aa smoked duck breast
- 5ml honey
- 2.5ml apple vinegar
- 15g tomato paste

Directions

18

1. Combine the duck with the other components in a bowl and stir.

2. Fill your air fryer machine with those contents, then cook for ten minutes on every side at 175°C

3.. After slicing the meat in half, divide it among plates and serve.

Recipes

MEAT

BBQ Chicken Cooked in Air Fryer

 **Cook time**
35 Minutes

 Servings: 4

Ingredients

- BBQ chicken (pre-cooked)
- One Provided Glaze

Directions

19

1. Set your air fryer's temperature to 149 °C. You can chop the chicken off the bone if it won't match your air fryer device.
2. Place the chicken inside the air fryer and cook it at 149° C for approximately 15 minutes. Make the glaze. Turn your chicken over and cover it with glaze.
3. Cook the chicken at 149° C for an additional 15 minutes. Check that your chicken is at least 63°C by using a meat thermometer.
4. Add more time if your chicken isn't heated sufficiently. Serve with carrots, mashed potatoes, or just about anything. Have fun!

Beef Prepared in Chinese Fashion

Cook time
25 MINS

Servings: 3

Ingredients

- 455g beef stew meat; cut into strips
- 30g sesame seeds; toasted
- 100g green onion; chopped

- 240ml soy sauce
- Five minced garlic cloves
- Black pepper

Directions

1. Place all of the components in an air fryer-compatible pan and stir well.
2. After placing the pan in the fryer device, cook it for around 20 minutes at 200°C.
3. Next, divide everything up into dishes and serve.

Meatballs Made from Lamb

Cook time
20 Minutes

Servings: 3

Ingredients

- 115g lamb meat; minced
- A whisked egg
- 4g oregano; chopped.
- 3g lemon zest
- Cooking spray
- Salt and black pepper

Directions

21

1. All the components, except the cooking spray, should be combined in a bowl and thoroughly mixed. Form the mixture into medium-sized meatballs.
2. After putting the meatballs in the basket of your air fryer appliance, coat them with cooking spray and cook for approximately 12 minutes at 205°C.
3. Next, divide among plates and serve.

Beef Kabobs Cooked in an Air Fryer

Cook time
40 Minutes

Servings: 5

Ingredients

- 455g beef chuck ribs cut in 1-inch pieces or any other tender cut meat- think nice steak, stew meat
- 80ml low-fat sour cream

- 30ml soy sauce
- A single peppers
- A half onion
- Eight 6-inch skewers

Directions

22

1. In a medium bowl, integrate soy sauce and sour cream. Put the beef pieces into the bowl and allow them to marinate for at least half an hour, preferably overnight.
2. Dice the onion and pepper into one-inch pieces.
3. After soaking wooden skewers in water for approximately ten minutes, thread peppers, onions, and meat onto the skewers.
4. Add a little bit of freshly grated pepper. Preheat the air fryer to 205°C.
5. Cook for around 10 minutes, rotating halfway through.

Beef with Arugula and Leeks

Cook time
22 Minutes

Servings: 3

Ingredients

- 455g ground beef
- 140g baby Rocket
- Three leeks; roughly chopped.

- 15ml olive oil
- 30ml tomato paste
- Salt and black pepper

Directions

23

1. Add the beef, leeks, oil, salt, and pepper to a pan that suits your air fryer appliance; toss to coat.

2. After placing the pan in the fryer, cook it for a minimum of 12 minutes at 195°C.

3. After that, add the Rocket and toss well. After dividing into bowls, serve.

Lamb Patties Made in an Air Fryer

Cook time
20 Minutes

Servings: 4

Ingredients

Lamb Burgers:
- 650 g Minced Lamb
- 10g Garlic Puree
- 5g Harissa Paste
- 10g Moroccan Spice
- Salt & Pepper

Greek Dip:
- 45g Greek Yoghurt
- 5g Moroccan Spice
- 2g Oregano
- A Small Lemon juice only

Directions

1. Place the lamb burger components in a mixing bowl and thoroughly combine until all of the lamb mince is properly seasoned.
2. Form the mince into lamb burger shapes with a burger press. Cook the lamb burgers in an air fryer appliance for 18 minutes at 180°C.
3. Make your Greek dip while they're cooking.
4. Mix the Grek dip ingredients with a fork and serve with your lamb burgers.

Recipes
SEAFOOD

Air Fryer Fish & Chips

Cook time
10 Minutes

Servings: 6

Ingredients

- Three to four pieces of cod or other white fish
- Two eggs
- 120g Plain flour

- 2g cajun seasoning or old bay
- salt and pepper to taste (cajun seasoning has salt already)

Directions

25

1. Place aside two eggs that have been beaten. Set aside a second bowl of flour. Set aside a mixture of panko crumbs and cajun seasoning in a different bowl.

2. Preheat the air fryer to 204°C for 5 minutes after spraying the air fry basket thoroughly.

3. Coat the fish in flour, followed by the egg mixture, and lastly in the panko mixture, and put it aside.

4. Do it with all the remaining fish pieces until they are coated. Cook the fish pieces in the air fryer for approximately 10 minutes at 204°C, turning them after 5 minutes.

5. When fish pieces vary in size and may impact cooking times, use a meat thermometer to ensure your fish is cooked to at least 63°C.

6. Serve and enjoy!

Rosemary Shrimp Kabobs

Cook time
13 Minutes

Servings: 3

Ingredients

- Eight shrimps; peeled and deveined
- Eight red pepper slices
- Four minced garlic cloves

- 15g chopped rosemary
- 15ml olive oil
- Salt and black pepper

Directions

26

1. Toss all of the components together in a mixing bowl. Thread two shrimp and two pepper slices onto a skewer, then add another two shrimp and two pepper pieces.
2. Thread two more shrimp and two pepper slices onto the other skewer, then repeat the process with the remaining two shrimp and two pepper slices.
3. Place the kabobs in the basket of your air fryer appliance, cook for 7 minutes at 180°C, and serve immediately with a side salad.

Air Fryer Tilapia

Cook time
12 Minutes

Servings: 3

Ingredients

- Two tilapia filets
- 30g Italian breadcrumbs
- 2g coarse sea salt
- An egg lightly beaten

Directions

27

1. Set up two plates and combine the breadcrumbs and salt in one.
2. On the other plate, place the beaten egg. Dip the tilapia fillet in the beaten egg, and follow in the breadcrumbs mix. Put in your air fryer.
3. Cook for approximately 12 minutes at 175°C and press the start button!

Roasted Cod and Parsley

Cook time
20 Minutes

Servings: 3

Ingredients

- Four medium cod filets; boneless
- A chopped shallot
- 1/4 cup butter; melted
- Two minced garlic cloves

- 12g parsley; chopped.
- 30ml lemon juice
- Salt and black pepper

Directions

28

1. In a mixing bowl, mix all of the elements except the fish; whisk thoroughly.

2. Apply this mixture to the fish fillets. Place them in your air fryer device and cook for 10 minutes at 200°C.

3. Serve the fish on plates.

Black Cod with Grapes, Fennel, Pecans and Kale

Cook time
25 Minutes

Servings: 2

Ingredients

- Two fillets of black cod
- salt and freshly ground black pepper
- 15ml olive oil
- 150g grapes halved

- A small bulb fennel sliced ¼-inch thick
- 60g pecans
- 100g shredded kale
- 12g white balsamic vinegar or white wine vinegar
- 30ml extra virgin olive oil

Directions

29

1. Begin by preheating the air fryer to 205°C. Season the cod fillets with pepper and salt, then pour, spritz, or smear them with olive oil. Put the fish in the air fryer basket, presentation side up (skin side down). 10 minutes in the air fryer. When the fish is done, transfer the fillets to a separate platter and tent gently with foil to rest. In a mixing bowl, combine the grapes, fennel, and pecans with a drizzle of olive oil, and season with salt and pepper. In the air fryer basket, combine the grapes, fennel, and pecans and cook for 5 minutes at 205°C, shaking the basket once throughout the frying time. Combine the pecans, grapes, and fennel in a mixing dish with the kale.

2. Dress the kale with the olive oil and balsamic vinegar, season with salt and pepper as you want, and serve with the cooked fish.

Coconut Shrimp

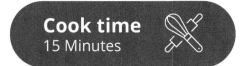

Cook time
15 Minutes

Servings: 3

Ingredients

- Twelve large shrimp; deveined and peeled
- 240ml coconut cream
- 5g parsley; chopped.

- 8g Cornflour
- Salt and black pepper

Directions

30

1. Toss the items in a pan that suits your air fryer.

2. Insert the pan into the fryer and cook for approximately 10 minutes at 180°C.

3. Serve immediately and enjoy!

Recipes

SIDE DISH

Air-Fryer Carrots

Cook time
30 Minutes

Servings: 4

Ingredients

- 455g baby carrots
- Two quartered small onions
- Three peeled garlic cloves, peeled
- 15ml olive oil

- 5ml white wine vinegar
- 2g dried thyme
- 2g salt
- 0.5g pepper
- Fresh thyme, optional

Directions

31

1. Heat the air fryer to 190°C. Toss the first 8 items in a large mixing bowl.

2. Put carrots in an air fryer basket on an oiled tray.

3. Cook, stirring sometimes, until carrots become crisp-tender, 18-20 minutes.

4. Sprinkle with fresh thyme, if preferred.

Yellow Squash and courgette

Cook time
40 Minutes

Servings: 2

Ingredients

- 455g courgettes; sliced
- A single yellow squash; halved, deseeded and cut into chunks
- 2g coriander; chopped.
- 22.5ml olive oil
- Salt and white pepper

Directions

32

1. Toss all of the components in a bowl and transfer them to the basket of your air fryer appliance.
2. Cook at 205°C for 35 minutes. Serve as a side dish, dividing everything among plates.

Air-Fryer Potato Wedges

Cook time
15 Minutes

Servings: 4

Ingredients

- Four russet potatoes (about 680g)
- 10ml rapeseed oil
- 60g grated Parmesan cheese
- 2g dried basil

- 5g seasoned salt
- 2g onion powder
- 2g garlic powder
- 1g pepper
- Prepared pesto, optional

Directions

33

1. Heat the air fryer to 205°C. Cut each potato in half lengthwise.

2. Each half should be cut into three wedges. Toss potatoes in a generous mixing bowl with oil to coat. Mix the remaining elements.

3. Toss with the potatoes to coat. Place your potato wedges in one layer on a greased tray in the basket of the air fryer.

4. Start the cooking process ook for 15-20 minutes, or until becomes golden brown and soft. Serve with pesto if preferred.

Air-Fryer Hash Browns

Cook time
15 MINS

Servings: 3

Ingredients

- A package (30 ounces) of frozen shredded hash brown potatoes
- A chopped large red onion, finely
- A finely chopped small sweet red pepper
- A finely chopped small green pepper

- Four minced garlic cloves
- 30ml olive oil
- 3g salt
- 3g pepper
- Three drops of hot pepper sauce, optional
- 10g minced fresh parsley

Directions

34

1. Begin heating your air fryer to 190°C. Mix the first eight elements in a generous mixing bowl; if you want, add spicy sauce.
2. Spread the combination in an equal 3/4-inch layer on a greased tray in the device's basket.
3. Cook for approximately 15–20 minutes, or until brown and crisp. Just before serving, top with parsley.

Moroccan Aubergine Dish

Cook time
20 MINS

Servings: 3

Ingredients

- 680g Aubergine; cubed
- 5g onion powder
- 3g. sumac

- 15ml olive oil
- 8ml Za'atar juice of a lime

Directions

35

1. Mix all of the components together in your air fryer appliance.

2. Begin the cooking process for 20 minutes at 175°C.

3. Serve as a side dish on individual plates.

Garlic Potatoes

Cook time
25 Minutes

Servings: 4

Ingredients

- Four large potatoes; pricked with a fork
- 30ml olive oil

- 15g minced garlic
- Salt and black pepper

Directions

36

1. In a mixing bowl, whisk all of the elements and thoroughly coat the potatoes.
2. Arrange the potatoes in your air fryer's basket and cook at 205°C for around 40 minutes.
3. Peel (if preferred), chop up, divide among plates, and serve as a side dish.

STARTER
Recipes

Fantastic Potato Chips

Cook time
15 Minutes

Servings: 5

Ingredients

- Two large potatoes
- Olive oil-flavored cooking spray
- 3g sea salt
- Minced fresh parsley, optional

Directions

37

1. First; preheat your air fryer device to 180°Celsius. Cut potatoes into extremely thin slices with a mandoline or vegetable peeler. Transfer to a helpful mixing bowl and add cold water to coat.
2. Soak for fifteen minutes before draining. Soak for another fifteen minutes with more cold water.
3. Drain the potatoes and wipe them dry with paper towels. Spritz the potatoes using cooking spray and season with salt. Arrange potato slices in one layer on an oiled tray in the air-fryer basket in batches.
4. Cook for 15–17 minutes, tossing and tossing each five to seven minutes, until crisp and golden brown.
5. Sprinkle with parsley if preferred.

Maple Parsnips

Cook time
40 Minutes

Servings: 2

Ingredients

- 907g parsnips; roughly cubed
- 5g chopped coriander

- 30ml olive oil
- 15ml maple syrup

Directions

38

1. In the beginning, preheat your air fryer device to 190°C before adding the oil and heating it up. Next, add the remaining elements and simmer for forty minutes.
2. Serve as a side dish on individual plates.

Runner Beans Roasted

Cook time
20 Minutes

Servings: 3

Ingredients

- 455g fresh runner beans, cut into 2-inch pieces
- 230g sliced fresh mushrooms
- A small red onion, halved and thinly sliced

- 30ml olive oil
- 3g Italian seasoning
- 2g salt
- 0.5g pepper

Directions

39

1. Prepare your air fryer to 190°C. Toss the components in a big mixing bowl to coat.

2. Arrange veggies in an air fryer basket on an oiled tray.

3. Begin the cooking process for eight to ten minutes, or until just tender. Toss to redistribute; cook until browned, an additional eight to ten minutes.

Mayo Brussels Sprouts

Cook time
20 Minutes

Servings: 2

Ingredients

- 455g Brussels sprouts; trimmed and halved
- 120g mayonnaise
- 30ml olive oil
- 30g minced garlic
- Salt and black pepper

Directions

1. Toss the sprouts with the salt, oil, and pepper in your air fryer.

2. Cook your sprouts for fifteen minutes at 200°C. Transfer to a mixing bowl and combine with the garlic and mayo. Serve as a side dish on individual plates.

Air-Fryer Plantains

Cook time
15 Minutes

Servings: 3

Ingredients

- Three minced garlic cloves
- 15g garlic salt
- 1/2 teaspoon onion powder
- Six green plantains peeled and cut into 1-inch slices
- Cooking spray

seasoning mix:
- 8g garlic powder
- 8g teaspoons garlic salt
- 2g onion powder
- 2g Sea salt
- Optional: Guacamole and pico de gallo

Directions

41

1. In a generous mixing bowl, combine the garlic, onion powder, and garlic salt. Cover with cold water and add plantains. Allow thirty minutes to soak. Drain the plantains and wipe them dry with paper towels. Heat up the air fryer to 180°Celsius. Arrange plantains in one layer on a greased tray in the air fryer basket in batches; spritz with cooking spray.

2. Cook for 10–12 minutes, or until gently browned. Sandwich the plantains between two sheets of aluminium foil. Flatten to 1/2-inch thickness using the bottom of a glass. Raise the temp of the air fryer to 205°C.

3. Return the flattened plantains to your air fryer and cook for another 2-3 minutes, or until golden brown. Combine the four spice mix components and sprinkle over the tostones. Optional ingredients can be added as desired.

Endives and Rice

Cook time
25 Minutes

Servings: 3

Ingredients

- 240ml veggie stock
- Four endives; trimmed and shredded
- Two chopped spring onions
- 120g white rice

- Three minced garlic cloves
- 15ml olive oil
- 5ml chilli sauce
- Salt and black pepper

Directions

42

1. Grease a pan that will suit your air fryer with the oil.

2. Toss with the remaining components. Set the pan in the air fryer appliance and cook for 20 minutes at 185°C.

3. Serve as a side dish by dividing everything across plates.

Recipes

VEGETABLE

Air-Fryer Baked Potato

Ingredients

- Four medium russet potatoes
- 30g softened butter
- Two minced garlic cloves, minced
- 2g salt

- 0.5g pepper
- Optional: Sour cream, butter, crumbled beef bacon, minced chives, guacamole, shredded cheddar cheese and minced fresh coriander

Directions

43

1. Start by heating your air fryer to 205°C. Clean potatoes and poke each with a fork many times. Combine the pepper, butter, salt, and garlic in a small bowl.
2. Rub the butter mixture over the potatoes. Wrap each with a piece of foil safely.
3. Put potatoes in an air fryer basket in one layer on a tray. Cook for 35–45 minutes, turning halfway through, until tender.

Simple Aubergine

Cook time
20 Minutes

Servings: 4

Ingredients

- Eight cubed baby Aubergines; cubed
- A chopped yellow onion
- A chopped bunch coriander
- A chopped green pepper

- 15g ml tomato sauce
- 2g garlic powder
- 15ml olive oil
- Salt and black pepper

Directions

44

1. Toss all of the components in a pan that matches your air fryer.

2. Transfer the pan to your air fryer and cook for approximately 10 minutes at 190°C.

3. Serve on individual plates.

Courgette Fries

Cook time
30 Minutes

Servings: 4

Ingredients

- Two medium courgette
- 120g panko bread crumbs
- 75g grated Parmesan cheese
- 5g smoked paprika
- 2g garlic powder

- 0.5g ground chipotle pepper
- 2g salt
- 0.5g pepper
- 40g Plain flour
- Two large eggs, beaten
- Cooking spray

Directions

45

1. Preheat the air fryer to 205°C. Half each courgette lengthwise and then crosswise.

2. Cut each piece into 1/4-inch slices lengthwise. Mix bread crumbs, cheese, and spices in a small bowl. Put the flour and eggs into different small bowls. Dip courgette slices in flour, followed by eggs, and lastly in the crumb mixture, patting to help the coating stick.

3. Arrange courgette on a greased tray in the air-fryer basket in batches; sprinkle with cooking spray.

4. Next, cook for about 8–10 minutes, turning midway, until golden brown.

Dill Corn

Ingredients

- Four ears of corn
- 30g melted. butter
- 6g chopped dill
- Salt and black pepper

Directions

46

1. Combine the salt, pepper, and butter in a mixing bowl.
2. Rub the corn with the butter mixture before placing it in the air fryer device.
3. Cook for roughly 6 minutes at 185°C. Divide the corn among plates, cover with the dill and serve.

Stuffed Sweet Potatoes

Ingredients

- Two medium sweet potatoes
- 5ml olive oil
- 240g cooked chopped spinach, drained
- 115g shredded cheddar cheese, divided
- Two cooked beef bacon strips, crumbled
- A green onion, chopped
- 240g fresh cranberries, coarsely chopped
- 80g chopped pecans, toasted
- 30g butter
- 1.5g Sea salt
- 0.6g pepper

Directions

1. Begin by preheating your air fryer machine to 205°C. Brush the potatoes with olive oil.

2. Set the tray in the basket of your air fryer machine.

3. Cook for around 30–40 minutes, or until potatoes become soft; cool slightly.

4. Half the potatoes lengthwise. Remove the pulp, leaving a 1/4-inch-thick shell behind.

5. Mash the potato pulp in a bowl; mix in the beef bacon, 3/4 cup cheese, butter, pepper, spinach, pecans, onion, cranberries, and salt. Spoon into potato shells, slightly mounding. Reduce the heat to 160°C.

6. Arrange potato halves on a tray inside your air fryer basket and cut them side up.

7. Cook for ten minutes. Cook until the remaining 1/4 cup cheese is melted, roughly one to two minutes.

Air-Fryer Red Potatoes

Ingredients

- 906g small unpeeled red potatoes, cut into wedges
- 30ml olive oil
- A tablespoon of minced fresh rosemary or a teaspoon of dried rosemary, crushed
- Two minced garlic cloves
- 2g salt
- 0.5g pepper

Directions

1. First, preheat the air fryer to 205°C.

2. Drizzle oil over the potatoes. Toss with salt, garlic, pepper, and rosemary to coat.

3. Set on an ungreased tray in an air-fryer basket.

4. Cook until potatoes become light brown and soft, 10-12 minutes, moving once.

Recipes

DESSERT

Strawberry Jam

Cook time
30 MINS

Servings: 2

Ingredients

- 455g chopped strawberries
- 800g sugar
- 480ml water
- Juice of two limes

Directions

49

1. Stir the strawberries with the sugar, lime juice, and water in a pan that matches your air fryer machine. Put the pan in the fryer and cook for approximately twenty-five minutes at 170°C.
2. Utilising an immersion blender, blend the mixture, then divide it into cups, refrigerate, and serve cool.

Pumpkin Cookies

Cook time
25 MINS

Servings: 4

Ingredients

- 375g flour
- 3g Bicarbonate of soda
- 120g pumpkin flesh; mashed
- 85ml honey
- 30g butter

- 5g vanilla extract
- 8g flax seed; ground
- 45ml water
- 85g dark chocolate chips

Directions

1. In a mixing bowl, merge flax seed and water; whisk and put aside for a few minutes. In another bowl, combine the salt, Bicarbonate of soda, and flour.
2. Combine butter, honey, pumpkin puree, vanilla essence, and flaxseed. Stir together the flour, honey mixture, and chocolate chips.
3. Scoop a single tablespoon of cookie dough onto a prepared baking sheet that suits your air fryer device, repeat with the remaining dough, place in your air fryer, and cook for approximately 15 minutes at 175 °C.
4. Allow the cookies to cool before serving.

Healthy Banana Bread

Cook time
40 Minutes

Servings: 3

Ingredients

- Three bananas; peeled and mashed
- Two whisked eggs
- 250g white flour
- 225g sugar
- A melted stick of butter
- 15g baking powder

Directions

1. Stir together all of the components in a mixing bowl.

2. Put this mixture in the air fryer in a prepared loaf pan.

3. Cook for 40 minutes at 170°C°. Allow the bread to cool before slicing, serving, and enjoying!

Creamy White Chocolate Cheesecake

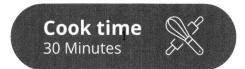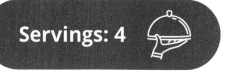
Ingredients

For the crust:
- 56g butter; melted
- 180g chocolate cookies; crumbled

For the filling:
- 680g cream cheese; softened
- 340g white chocolate; melted
- 200g sugar
- Three whisked eggs
- 120g Double cream
- 15g Cornflour
- 12g vanilla extract

Directions

1. In a mixing bowl, merge the butter and cookie crumbs.
2. On a prepared cake pan with parchment paper, sprinkle the cookie crumbs in the bottom and freeze for now.
3. In an additional bowl, mix together all of the other items. Spread the mixture over the cake crust, place it in the fryer, and cook for twenty minutes at 160°C.
4. Let the cake cool before setting it in the fridge for a full hour before serving.

Plum Bars Recipe

Cook time
25 Minutes

Servings: 4

Ingredients

- 340g dried plums
- 200g rolled oats
- 200g Light brown sugar
- 2.5g Bicarbonate of soda

- 90ml water
- 30g butter; melted
- 1 egg; whisked
- 2.5g cinnamon powder
- Cooking spray

Directions

53

1. Using a food processor, blend plums and water and pulse until a sticky spread is formed.
2. In a mixing bowl, combine egg, cinnamon, oats, sugar, Bicarbonate of soda, and butter, and stir thoroughly. Spread half of the oats mix in a baking pan that suits your air fryer device and has been coated with cooking oil, then top with the other half of the oats mix.
3. Insert into your air fryer and cook for approximately 16 minutes at 175°C.
4. Allow the mixture to cool before cutting it into medium bars and serving.

Cherry Cream Pudding

Cook time
60 Minutes

Servings: 3

Ingredients

- 360g cherries; pitted and halved
- 360g whipping cream
- 70g raisins

- 50g sugar
- 90g chocolate chips.
- Four egg yolks

Directions

54

1. Put all of the components in a bowl for mixing.

2. Move the mixture to a well-greased air fryer pan.

3. Start the cooking process for fifty-five minutes at 155°C.

   Allow to cool before serving.

Printed in Great Britain
by Amazon

36529807R00044